THE NUDE
IN
IMPRESSIONISM

PARK
LANE

The Nude in Impressionism

In 1863, Edouard Manet exhibited *Luncheon on the Grass* at the "Salon des Refusés".

This event not only marked a complete rupture with the past, but also the first revolutionary representation of the nude, in strong contrast with the traditional schemes which had remained fixed for such a long time.

The artististic spheres of Paris constituted the background for these changes. In fact, in the course of the XIXth century, the capital played an important part, similar to that of Florence in the XVth century or Rome in the XVIIth century.

It was in Paris that artists from all over the world met, eager to improve their studies with the great Masters, or to take part in the conversations which animated the cafés. How did this rupture with tradition come about? Which steps, which changes had occured?

According to the Masters, the nude was "et principium et fons", a formula which had not been challenged until the advent of what was to be known as the Modern School.

Théodore Géricault (1791-1824) was the first to claim the necessity of freedom in creation which was to ring like the heralding of a new poetics. In contrast with the smooth, uniform painting of the neo-classic period he was to oppose an impetuous style, that of the magnificent painting of *Naked Woman, Standing* (plate 3), which anticipates with surprising penetration a certain period in Cézanne's painting. Géricault has constructed the body through a whole set of skilful snatches, thus setting off all the strength of a drawing submitted to a rigorous composition.

During the first half of the XIXth century the most important conservative painter had been Jean-Auguste-Dominique Ingres (1780-1867). A disciple of David's, whose admiration for the classical world he shared, he never grew tired of strongly recommending the utmost precision in the study of reality.

One of his first paintings, the portrait of *La Belle Zélie*, already pointed him out as one of the greatest exponents of feminine nude. With *The Valpinçon Bather* (plate 2) and the famous *Odalisque* (plate 1), his figures reached a sort of mellow languor, supported by the masterly manner in which he modelled the shapes and by the sharpness and harmony of his composition. But, as Delacroix said, his works and those of his pupils never contained "a fragment of the truth that comes from the soul". Those artists never derived their inspiration either from the love of nature or from a careful observation of life.

Eugène Delacroix (1798-1863) could not stand the innumerable reminders of the Greeks or of the Romans, just as he refused the academic canons or the constant imitation of classic statuary. In his opinion colour was more important than the drawing, and fantasy came before technique. Whereas for Ingres and his school Poussin and Raphael were fixed benchmarks, young Delacroix had chosen Rubens and the Venetian painters.

1 – Jean-Auguste-Dominique Ingres. *Odalisque* – 1814. Musée du Louvre, Paris.

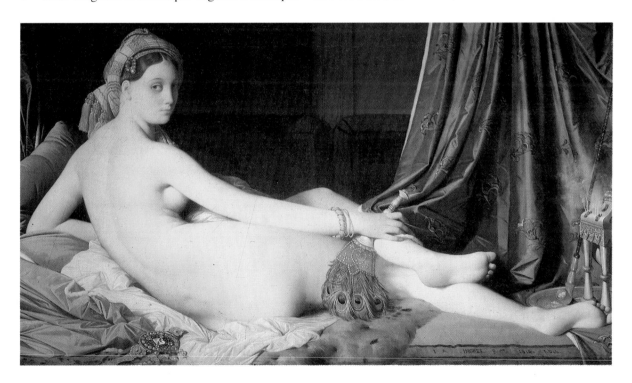

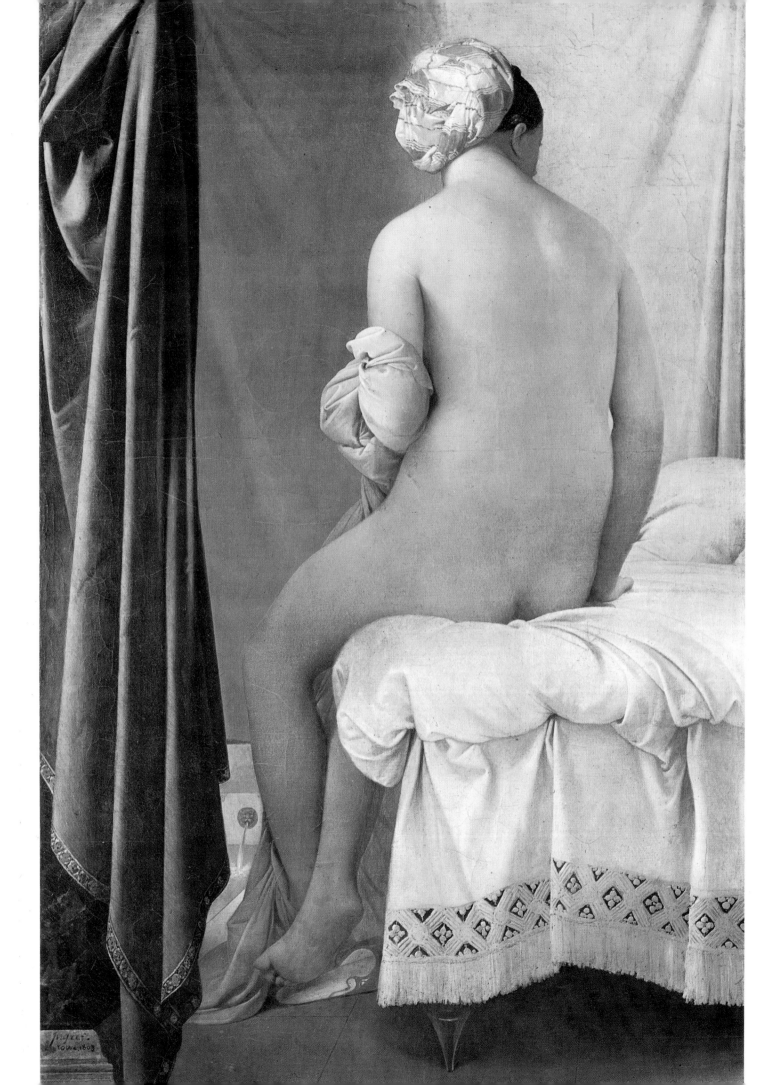

2 – Jean-Auguste-
Dominique Ingres.
*The Valpinçon
Bather* – 1808.
Musée du Louvre,
Paris.

3 – Théodore Géricault.
*Naked Woman,
Standing*. Musée des
Beaux-Arts, Rouen.

Marietta — à Rome

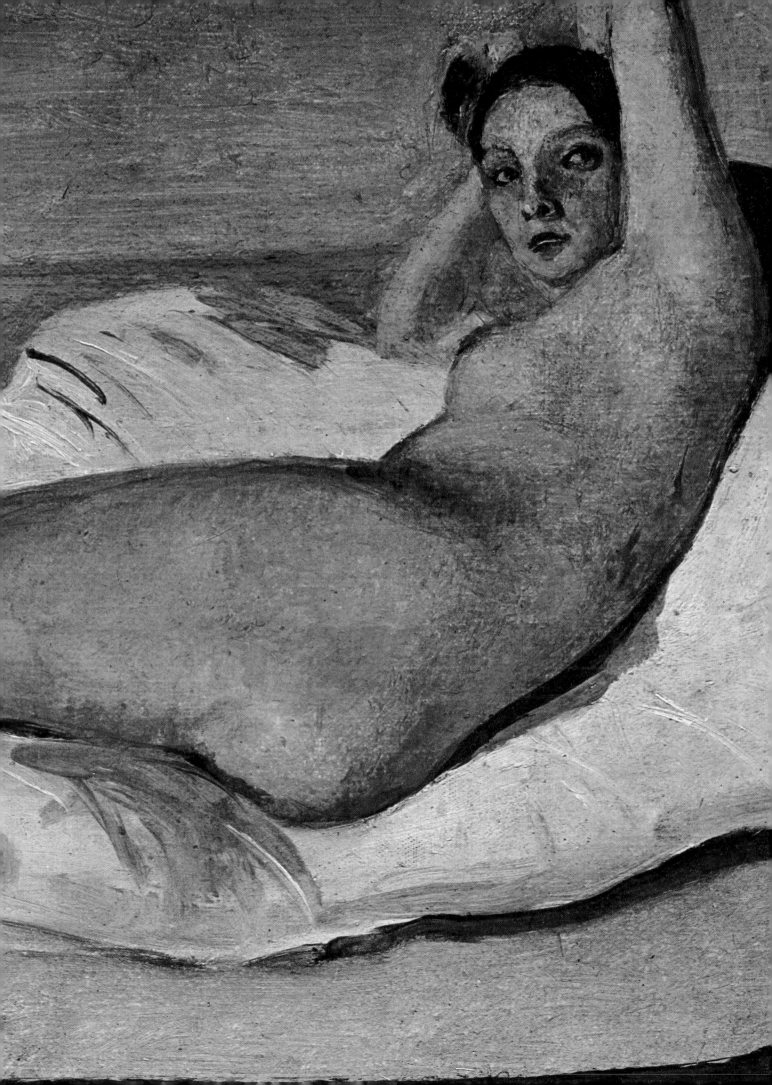

5 – Gustave Courbet. *The Studio of the Painter* (detail) – 1854-55. Musée d'Orsay, Paris.

Despising tradition he composed his paintings in the shape of an inverted triangle, like in the *Massacre at Chios*, in which the bare and slaughtered bodies are not modelled in the varied shades of chiaroscuro. The subject itself was neither patriotic nor edifying. In order to create a light effect, he touches the arms of the old woman with shades of pink, orange, yellow and light blue; he will go as far as writing down in his diary that the lack of tension in his paintings is due to the uniformity of the colour. The preliminary sketches for *The Death of Sardanapalus* have undoubtedly been the starting point for a new way of painting. Delacroix left the generation which came after him his conception of colour, which he largely derived from Constable. He substituted

movement for stable equilibrium and the manner in which he dealt with colours cleared the way for the Impressionists' experimentations. His eliminating of earth colours and the manner in which he used the pure tones makes it possible to assert that he heralds the coming of the Impressionists.

Jean-Baptiste-Camille Corot (1796-1875) also played an important part in the formulation of Impressionism, as he taught how to do without false shades and artificially darkened tones. He had left aside every artifice typical of the Renaissance style and replaced them by flat spaces and luminous surfaces, as can be seen especially in the studies he did between 1840 and 1863.

The *Roman Odalisque* (also called *Marietta*, plate 4) dates

6 – Gustave Courbet. *The Three Bathers* – 1868. Musée du Petit Palais, Paris.

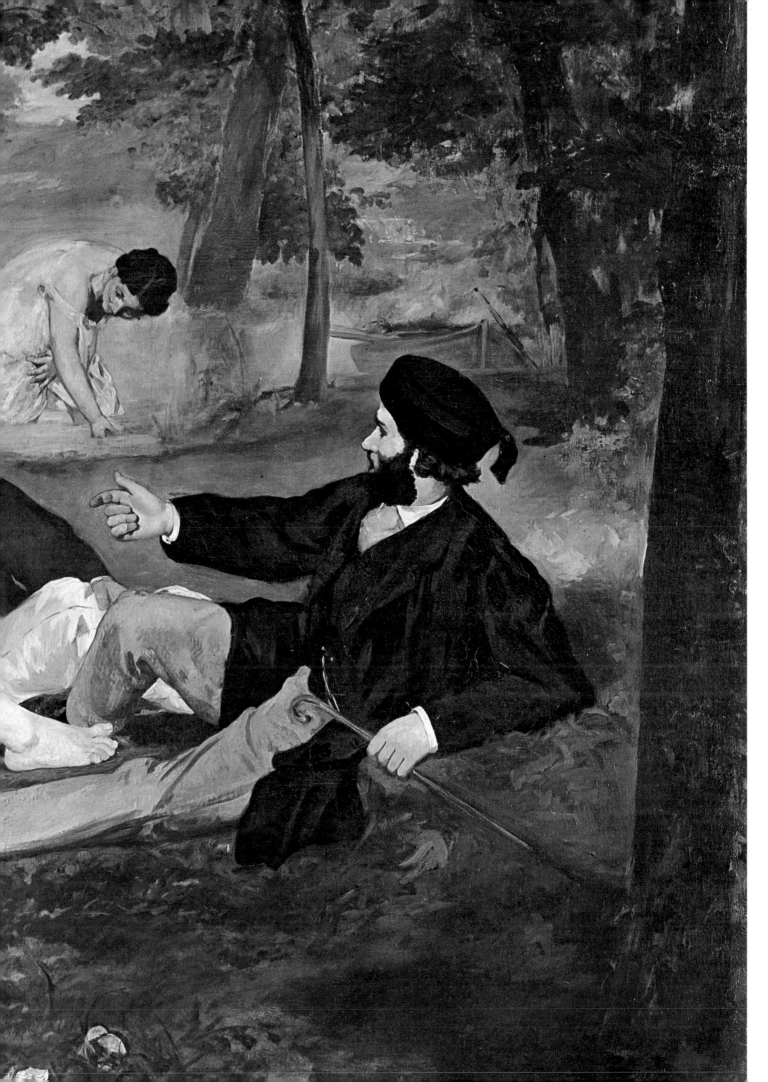

back to this period, in which he reaches a kind of mysterious sensual pleasure. He did not come to the point of splitting up light into its constituent colours, but he organized and simplified forms in order to obtain a classical model. However, his insistence on precision and the search after truth bears a great resemblance to the Impressionists' ideals.

The next step concerns the conventions that govern the choice of the subject. Up to that time, only the characters considered as "dignified" were represented in the various art schools. The peasant, the man in the street, women combing their hair, looking at themselves in a mirror or captured in a particular moment of their everyday life, were doomed to being a part of what was known as "subject picture", or not being a part of anything.

During the 1848 revolution, a group of artists settled in the village of Barbizon, to study nature with a different eye. Gustave Courbet (1819-1877) was the one who named this movement, after a one-man exhibition which took place in 1855 in Paris: "Realism, G. Courbet". What characterized his figures were his scorn for the stagy mannerism of official art as well as his desire to scandalize the bourgeoisie of the time. Courbet became an unleashing force for the Impressionists. He taught them not to fear the apparently unpretentious subjects and never tired of repeating that painting was fundamentally a concrete form of art which consisted in representing real things.

Courbet has painted several bathers or sleepers in the nude. In his picture *The Studio of the Painter* (plate 5), one can admire a woman standing naked behind the artist, showing her strong and splendid body painted in delicate shades.

The history of painting during the XIXth century differs entirely from that which preceded it. In the past, indeed, offices and responsibilities were only bestowed on confirmed artists whose celebrity could not but grow.

On the contrary, in the XIXth century, there came to exist a gulf between the so-called best-selling painters and the anti-

8 – Edouard Manet. *Jupiter and Antiope* – 1856. Private collection.

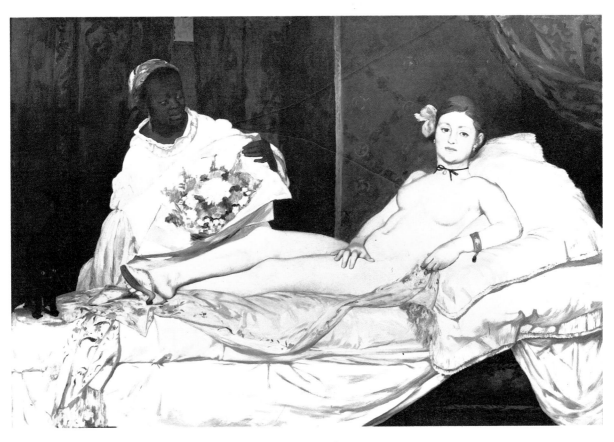

9 – Edouard Manet. *Olympia* – 1863. Musée d'Orsay, Paris.

conformists, who generally got to be appreciated after they had died. And thus we have reached this rupture from tradition which had initially been attributed to Edouard Manet but which, in our opinion, must also be granted to all the artists who took Courbet's lesson seriously.

Before Manet, painters had their models pose in their studios, exposing them to a carefully calculated light. In order to suggest volume and a certain consistency, they moved gradually from light to shade. To draw, they took their inspiration from the models of statues and, following the established technique, they idealized Raphael's and Guido Reni's famous examples. They were mostly anxious to make volumes "turn" so as to obtain subtle shades of colours; they reproduced the nacreous sheen of the flesh through light strokes of green and blue. The public had now grown accustomed to the figures represented in that way, oblivious of the fact that, in the open air, it was impossible to capture the tones which mark the transition between light and shade, because of the fact that in the sunshine the contrasts are more marked, the volumes are less exalted, the parts on which light falls are not so bright as they are in a studio and the shades are never uniformly grey or black.

The great artists had created a convincing representation of the visible world which Manet and his disciples completely upset by provoking in chromatics a revolution similar to that which the Greeks had undertaken in the treatment of forms. But what was it exactly that the Impressionists had discovered? That when you observed nature you did not see well-defined objects, with a precise shape, but rather some mixed tonalities. Edouard Manet (1832-1883) very boldly suppressed dimmed lighting, which explains why his paintings were refused at the 1863 Salon. However, in the face of the enormous hue and cry which ensued, the jury was compelled to create a special exhibition for the paintings they had refused which went by the name of "Salon des Refusés". And there it was that the cause for all that scandal was shown: *Luncheon on the Grass* (plate 7). Both critics and public unanimously declared that this stark naked woman sitting between two men was highly indecent. Instead of a complicated light which would have lent itself to multiple chromatisms, Manet opted for a garish, level, dazzling light, with the result that pure flat tones and clear-cut outlines replaced every manner of hue. The feminine figure is not achieved through a gradation of shades and reflections, but created by the very colour. This quick and essential vision aimed at a truer representation of reality.

Jupiter and Antiope (plate 8), one of his first paintings from 1856, already testimonied to a certain change, although it still

13

10 – Edouard Manet. *Brunette with Naked Breasts* – 1872 ca. Private collection.

11 – Edouard Manet. *Blonde Semi-nude* – 1875. Musée d'Orsay, Paris.

had a mythological theme. The scandal was to break out two years later when Manet exhibited *Olympia* (plate 9) at the 1865 Salon. It was a complete innovation both from the aesthetic and the pictorial point of view. Manet's nude apparently lacked any finishing retouch of the drawing. The figure is painted boldly, without any attempt at softening curves or angles. The harsh light of the picture is that of the body whose shapes are enhanced by a faint line. Not a shade of pink or amber on the monochromous skin: other bright colours provide the contrast. With the *Brunette with Naked Breasts* (1872, plate 10) and the *Blonde Semi-nude* (plate 11) the same discourse is continued, the colour is applied with light white and red strokes in order to render the sheen of the nude, then the body is dealt with according to the immediate sensation it creates on the artist.

With *Olympia*, the French school is given a fresh start. At this stage, a clarification on a point of social order becomes necessary if we expect to understand what was being transgressed and the sharp criticism which was being directed at the new movements. At that time the number of people who were interested in art grew considerably. Previously art had been a matter for the sole intellectuals, artists and scholars. The interval between the Salons grew lesser and lesser and few pictures were exhibited. In 1855 the Universal Exhibition had given rise to the construction of an immense palace

which, from then on, was to house a yearly Salon. The lower middle classes and even the working classes were thus in a condition to have a direct contact with the works of the great painters, those very social classes who were to criticize and reject violently Manet's *Olympia*. Lacking any culture or past, but strengthened by the social position it had acquired thanks to the industrial and commercial prosperity, this new class has, in a way, originated a decadence of taste. The history of modern painting, and particularly that which is linked with the nude, must therefore be analysed from that point of view as well.

The radical changes which Manet brought about were to win the approval of a large group of artists, among which were Renoir, Monet, Pissarro and Sisley. Those are the names linked with the "First Impressionism". The most important thing, beyond the innumerable anecdotes concerning the origins of that school, are the general theories of Impressionist painting which one can summarize in these few words: nothing in nature has a particular colour. The light tones down everything differently, according to its intensity and the way in which it strikes the object. The light which is split up by the prism is also broken up by the artist into small brightly tinted spots. In this way it becomes possible to obtain more lively tonalities than those of the mixed colours. The analysis which the Impressionists have carried out on light will result in obtaining three primary colours: blue, yellow and red. The

12 – Pierre-Auguste
Renoir.
*Little Blue
Nude* – 1879.
Albright-
Knox Art Gallery.
Buffalo.

13 – Pierre-Auguste
Renoir. *The Blond
Bather* – 1881-82.
Private collection.

other three colours are complementary, in order of precedence, orange, violet and green. These prismatic colours are more or less the only ones to be used by the painter; in addition, he sometimes uses black to reproduce the absence of light and white to soften tints. As a rule he only mixes two primary colours at a time. He no longer aims at interpreting a theme directly or expressly, but rather at fixing the impression it provokes on him. Apart from Renoir, the members of the first Impressionist group will not be particularly interested in the nude.

Monet will paint a few nudes in his youth, which reflect the influence of Corot and Courbet, but thereafter he will mainly be interested in landscapes. The same goes for Sisley and Pissarro. It is just the opposite for Renoir, whose famous sentence "If God had not created the woman's flesh I would never have become a painter", is a good synthesis of the love with which he pictures women in the nude.

When he was still hesitating for a personal style, Renoir (1841-1919) was influenced by Courbet, as can be seen in his picture *Diana* which dates back to 1867. At that time, follow-

ing the example set by Courbet, every painter used a palette knife. His picture *Nude, Sunshine Effect*, painted in 1876, can be considered as a "nude-programme" of the new school. The model seems to be immersed in nature. The patches of shade which project onto the surrounding greenery weave patterns on her skin and Renoir has solved the problem by using mauve tints. The outline of the face almost disappears, the whole picture is more than ever anticonformist and daring. The *Little Blue Nude* (plate 12) was painted in 1879 and *The Blond Bather* (plate 13) was painted in Naples in 1882, during a journey in Italy. The influence of Raphael, whose works Renoir had admired in Rome, is clearly visible in this painting, and so is that of the Pompei frescoes, although the picture is more admirable for its cold luminosity than for its sensuality. In 1882 Renoir conceived the idea of a large-size painting, the protagonists of which were to be a group of young women bathers on the banks of a river (plate 14). He was to start working on it when he came back from his Italian trip and finished it in 1887. This long gestation is due to the various preparatory studies which Renoir did in several steps. For the

14 – Pierre-Auguste Renoir. *The Large Bathers* – 1887.
 Museum of Art, Mrs C.S. Tyson Collection, Philadelphia.

theme the painter had drawn his inspiration from François Gilardon's famous bas-relief which ornamented the Boulevard des Marmousets pond in Versailles. The outlines of the painting, neat and precise, give it an ornamental aspect notwithstanding a certain joy of living. The bathers of that period greatly differ from those which he painted at the beginning of 1900. As they are immersed in a translucent atmosphere their aspect is somewhat unreal, and there often remains a slight hint of hardness about them. Bound as it was to the atmospheric aspect of the world, the Impressionists' vision could not really find an echo in Renoir's peculiar temperament, and his love for sculptural plasticity. That severe hardness did not fit the humour of a man who was a lover of sunshine and light. Many years later, having forsaken that excessive rigour, Renoir will finally attain a maturity devoid of any marked influence and will succeed in forging his characteristical style. From now on and until his death, he will paint bathers who do not bathe in water but rather in light. If the pictures he painted around 1890 are still transition works, they nevertheless testimony to his current evolution. They mark the stage when he abandoned his so-called

15 – Pierre-Auguste Renoir. *Sketch for "The Large Bathers"* – 1884-85. Mr Paul Pétridès Collection, Paris.

16 – Pierre-Auguste Renoir. *Bather Sitting on a Rock* – 1892. Private collection.

"période aigre" for another type of Impressionism, entirely different from anything which had preceded it.

As they are no longer bound by the contour lines which isolated them, the forms are modelled in long supple strokes which come together and blend, whereas the Impressionist brush-stroke remained extraneous, in a way. Renoir also found a solution to the alternative form-light, with a pictorial formula which does not hamper the construction of the form (see his *Bather Sitting on a Rock*, 1892, plate 16).

One can hardly go wrong when saying that he painted life in its constant flux, following the great rhythm of nature, that mysterious logic which binds every living being together.

Having by now grown old and suffering from rheumatism, Renoir did not give up painting. From his first to his last picture, his love for light never diminished but kept growing.

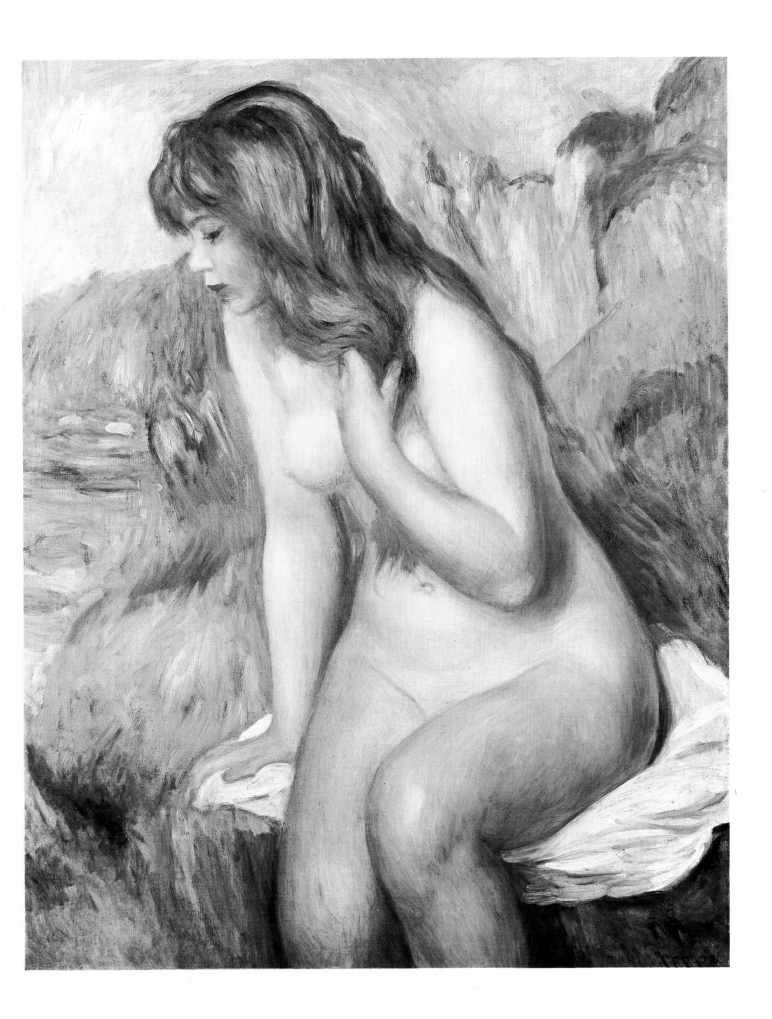

17 – Pierre-Auguste Renoir. *Seated Bather* – 1914.
The Art Institute of Chicago.

18 – Pierre-Auguste Renoir. *Madeleine Bruno* or *The Two Bathers* (detail) – 1916. Private collection.

In his last paintings, he uses a richer matter and he coats his canvas with velvety patches, while his palette turns back to lighter tones.

The bathers which constitute the main theme of his late works (*Madeleine Bruno* or *The Two Bathers*, plate 18), the odalisques or the laundresses cannot be separated from the other elements whose essence they share and to which they are intimately linked. Whatever the theme he tackles, Renoir constructs the elements around spots of light.

At that time, Eugène Chevreul, a scientist, started an extensive study of the chromatic harmonies. His work *Principles of Colour Harmony and Colour Contrast and Their Application in Art* was published in 1839. In this treatise, Chevreul asserted that contiguous colours will influence and modify one another. He also affirmed that any single colour is surrounded by the feeble halo of its complementary colour. This scientist, who was also interested in optical blending, found out that, seen from a distance, woollen threads of different mixed colours tended to be perceived as a uniform colour.

The Impressionists had first-hand knowledge of Chevreul's work, and the theory of optical blending caused them to give the shade the colour which was complementary to that of the object which projected it. They superimposed the colours upon the canvas so that the eye would blend them and create tonalities which were more intense than those obtained by their mere combination on the palette. The fundamental difference between Georges Seurat (1859-1891) and the artists who preceded him, and especially the Impressionists, is precisely his great interest for the chromatic solutions of light suggested by the scientists. Lonely, Seurat met with a premature death at the age of 32, but he read Chevreul's lesson as an indispensable course. Very early he started to draw in black and white and, having become a master in tonality contrast, he treated the colours in the same way, applying to them the laws of contrast. His pictures are not so bright as those of the Impressionists, they are painted in big flat strokes and resemble mosaics. What they lose in vivacity, they gain in balance and harmony. The separation of the elements, the reciprocal reactions of the neighbouring colours give them a rare value of luminous and colourful synthesis.

Seurat has painted nudes by pure chance. On the other hand, his Neo-Impressionist theory is somewhat too strict to allow a representation of the nude which, from a strictly structural point of view, requires a bold escape from the rules. What he has left us can give us an idea of what modern nude has lost when he prematurely died. In *Bathing at Asnières* (1883-84,

plate 19), the atmosphere we breathe in is transparent and vibrating, the surface seems to flicker, earth colours are predominant and the spectacle of reality commands attention regardless of any cultural reference. Seurat connects the figures he studies separately and matures the Impressionists' lesson, fully conscious of the role of the subject in his rela-

19 – Georges Seurat. *Bathing at Asnières* – 1883-84.
The Tate Gallery, London.

23

tionship with the world. He has always remained true to his temperament, that of a painter who was fascinated by the play of light. That is why he has always been attracted by the sea which accentuated this aspect of vision.

Between 1887 and 1888 he paints *Girls Posing* (plate 20), a picture in which he introduces a new chromatic luminosity. In the *Seated Nude, Profile* (1886-87, plate 21), which he will later include in a slightly different form in *Girls Posing*, (the above-mentioned picture), the outlines, rather than defining the object, seem to indicate the lines of force of light waves, a technique that Boccioni will use a few years later. In that

20 – Georges Seurat. *Girls Posing* (small version) – 1888. Berggruen Collection, Paris.

21 – Georges Seurat. *Seated Nude, Profile, Study for "The Models"* – 1886-87. Musée d'Orsay, Paris.

26

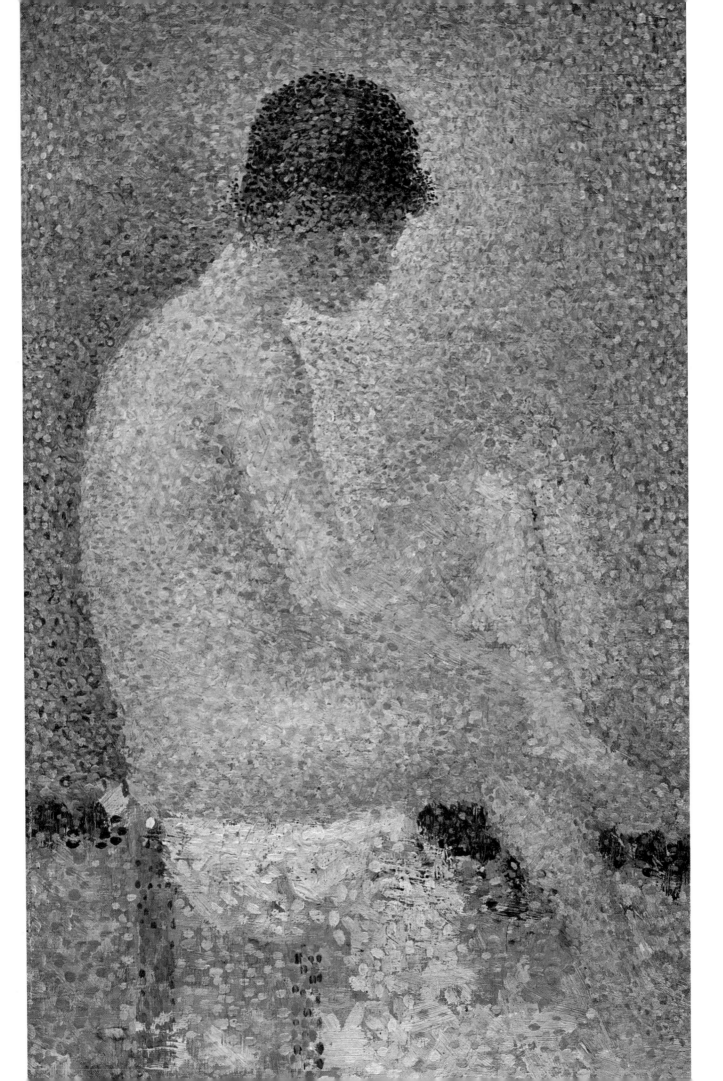

22 – Paul Cézanne. *A Modern Olympia* – 1872-74. Musée d'Orsay, Paris.

painting, as is the case in some others, a light halo provides an outline for the figure. In *Standing Nude*, another study for *Girls Posing*, the whole picture seems to be composed of scales of light.

Thanks to the Impressionists the life of a woman, in its most common aspects and in the course of a peaceful humdrum existence, undergoes a period of important evolution. The latter however concerns the means of painting, not its ends and perhaps it is this very improvement of the technique which causes some artists to waver.

The first to feel strongly that a new type of problems has just come about is Paul Cézanne (1839-1906). Right from the start his favourite form was colour. In his conversations with his friend, the writer Emile Zola, he used to quote Rubens,

Veronese and Rembrandt. What he mostly liked about Veronese were his voluptuous coloured volumes and the luminous atmosphere. The beginning of the artistic career of the future creator of plastic forms is dominated by a kind of romanticism. His art ripens among intellectual and sensual conflicts, in a succession of expectations and dramatical despondency. Beside the explicitly sensual expression of his nudes his romantic style reveals the painter's pure sensitivity. It is his romanticism which enables him to exteriorize his inmost feelings. Following the suggestion of his friend and adviser Pissarro, he takes part in the first exhibition of the impressionist group in 1874. His picture *A Modern Olympia* (plate 22), which he painted at doctor Guichet's, is a brilliant composition, full of light, which is still related to the roman-

23 – Paul Cézanne. *The Eternal Feminine* – 1875-77. Private collection.

tic vein but modernized by the memory of Manet's famous picture. Disgusted by the way his paintings had been criticized, he was to retire to l'Estaque in 1878.

Contrarily to the other artists, his social position enabled him not to look for someone who would buy his pictures, and so he devoted all his life to the task of trying to reach the perfection he had assigned to himself. "To do Poussin again after nature" was his motto. What he meant was that the Classicists like Poussin had reached a marvellous harmony and balance. Nothing was left to chance in their compositions. Their bodies had a firm and solid look. This was the kind of art Cézanne aimed at but, in order to reach his goal, he was compelled to change his technique. As he edged away from Impressionism, the new discoveries he made gave rise

to the desire to reach the sense of order of which Poussin had become a master. The Impressionists' pictures were undoubtedly full of light, but they were chaotic. Now, just as Cézanne refused any type of return to the academic conventions, he also refused any tendency to "confusion", and just as his colours were intense, he also had a desire for neat compositions. For their part, the Impressionists applied their colours separately, having given up the habit of mixing them on their palettes, with the result that their paintings had an intense light about them. Cézanne wanted to go further still. His strenuous researches and his constant love for painting were to lead him to a conception of pure, refined colour. By depriving the subject he had elected to paint from the lines which defined it, by balancing the volumes through a series of coloured

24 – Paul Cézanne. *Five Bathers* – 1885-87. Kunstmuseum, Basel.

researches, he was to create a kind of chromatic geometry. Timid, violent and touchy, Cézanne was to shy away from women throughout his whole life. He dreamt of having his naked model pose for him immersed in nature. Wishful thinking, since women put him off, not so much for fear of giving rise to the gossip of the provincial milieu in which he lived, but rather through an excess of modesty. When he discovered Delacroix he wrote: "It is the first time someone has expressed himself through volumes since the Great Masters' time." His *Nudes on the Shore*, which he painted in 1870, date back from the period which immediately followed.

At the beginning, his evocations, such as *The Eternal Feminine* (1875-77, plate 23), conveyed a spectacular sensuality. But these works contained neither order nor discipline nor architecture. The matter, which already dominates the theme, is often slightly empty. A comparison between his first compositions and the preparatory studies for his picture *The Love Struggle* reveals the ground he has covered. The slightly exacerbated sensuality yields to a plastic sensuality, where his research for coloured volumes is subordinated to his desire of composition. Rhythm prevails, the concept of structure is asserting itself. Thus he turns away from the allegories to which the first nudes had been bound, and starts painting directly onto his canvas, refusing any manner of preliminary drawing, as in the *Three Bathers* of 1876. In the *Five Bathers* (1885-87, plate 24), his need for architectural balance is obvious. This theme, one of the artist's favourite, enables him to develop the principle of construction through colour. A composition which seems to have been drawn reveals that in fact Cézanne shapes his forms with a brush.

For him, the problem of the nude is linked with that of composition. While he juxtaposes tonalities with the sole scope of creating volumes, he puts the human body on the

25 – Paul Cézanne. *Standing Female Nude* – 1895 ca. Musée du Louvre, Paris.

same footing as the surfaces and the masses. And when he unifies the various elements to give his picture a monumental nature his nudes nevertheless retain graceful attitudes. In order "to do Poussin after nature", he imparts a sort of inexpressible but truly admirable lyricism to his models. His bathers, which he sets very simply under some trees or on some river banks, blend totally with nature. Haunted as he is by the harmony which every sculpture contains in itself and which Poussin had already sensed in nature, he associates the movements of the busts and arms with the majestic volumes of the trees, the regularity of the corn-fields, the clouds that form magnificent architectures in the sky. In these compositions the human beings wrestle on the grass of the meadows or immerse into the water of a stream, under the cover of the greenery.

Mankind yearning for purification? That may be! Anyhow, for the spectator, the reference smacks of paganism.

Some have said that his bodies were misshapen. But if deformity there is, it merely expresses torment and a constant refusal of idealization, and from this conflict the figure emerges purified. In the *Bathers*, mainly those of his last pictures, *Nymphs by the Sea* (1890-94, plates 26 and 27), there is absolutely no sex appeal. Whereas in Renoir every-

27 – Paul Cézanne. *Nymphs by the Sea* (right side) – 1890-94. Musée du Louvre, Paris.

thing is carnal fervour, Cézanne elects bodies that are modelled by abstract colours. Indeed it is in his last works that a true renovation becomes evident and he attains a sort of abstraction in his colours, which have now become free from any technical or aesthetical preoccupation.

The Large Bathers (plate 28), on which he worked for about seven years, from 1898 to 1905, can be considered as his spiritual will. The picture is built according to pyramidal rhythms that multiply and intersect. In the geometrical appearance Cézanne sees the pure expression of the essence of the shapes. This pyramidal theme intends to represent the emotion of man in front of the ascension of matter into the immensity of space. *The Large Bathers* follow a rhythm of parallel lines that would meet if their impetus was not blocked on the edge of the canvas. The whole picture is bathed in a bluish atmosphere representing the light-space. From now on he will apply his colours more lightly instead of juxtaposing the various coats as he used to do, with the result that his pictures will take on the lightness of a watercolour. The joints of the models seem knotted, their shapely and muscular limbs, their breasts and the folds of their hips are but formulae.

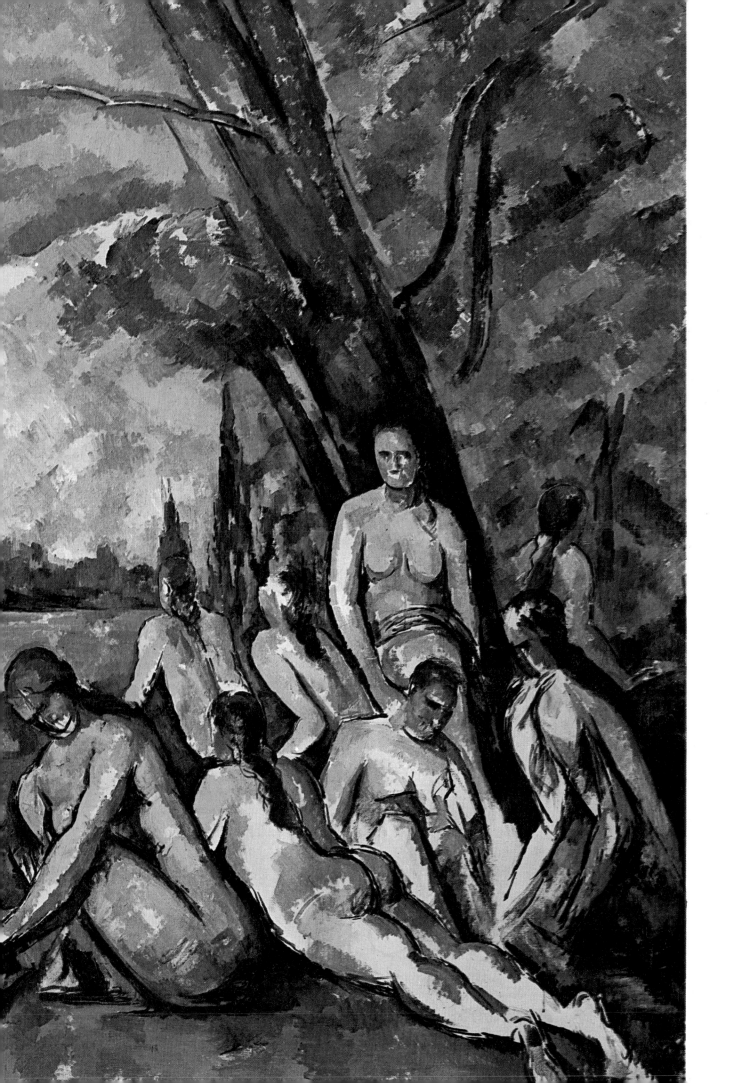

29 – Paul Gauguin. *The Yellow Christ* – 1889. Albright-Knox Art Gallery, Buffalo.

30 – Paul Gauguin. *The Green Christ (Breton Calvary)* – 1889. Musées Royaux des Beaux-Arts de Belgique, Brussels.

The mystery of Cézanne's nudes remains unfathomable. Having by now totally mastered his art, he reduces his palette to two essential colours, blue and orange-ochre, alternating them with half-tints, which he applies in successive gradations. Therein lies Cézanne's greatness: when he decided to start all over again, as if no other type of painting had existed before him, refusing to accept any traditional pictorial technique as final. His indifference for "accurate drawing" and his attempt to sacrify the traditional accuracy of the contents will cause a deep change in the history of art.

Quite different is Gauguin's case (1848-1903). Between 1883 and 1903, the years which are judiciously considered as the best for Cézanne's painting, Gauguin was discovering an unknown world. Indeed, this former stockbroker was to start painting late in life after having taught himself practically everything. His unquestioned master was Pissarro who cancelled ochre, earth colours and black from the neophyte's paintbox. During his stay at Pont-Aven, in Brittany, Gauguin was to paint *The Yellow Christ* (1889, plate 29). In this remote part of France the painter was to rediscover the sense of the

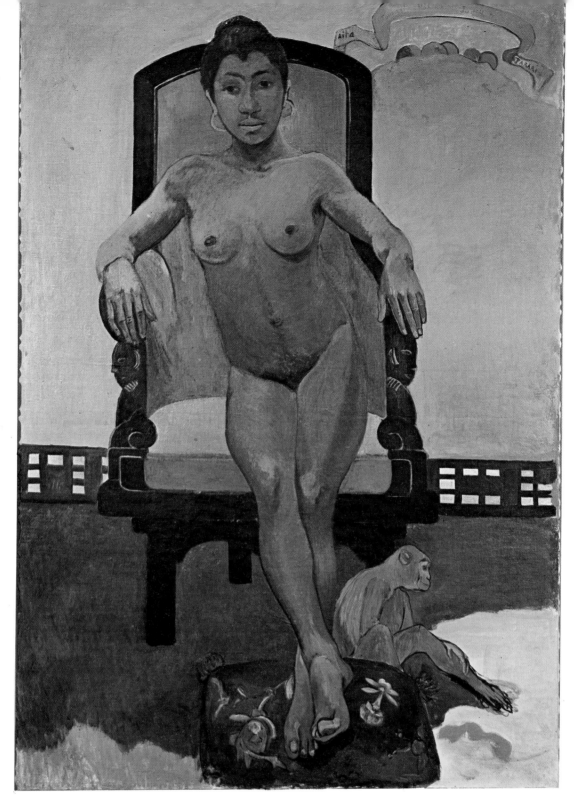

31 – Paul Gauguin. Annah yhe Javanese ("*Aita Tamari Vahine Judith Te Parari*") – 1893-94. Private collection.

32 – Paul Gauguin. *Two Tahitian Women* – 1899.
The Metropolitan Museum of Art,
Gift of William Church Osborn, 1949, New York.

pagan idol, for here Christ is not so much a religious subject as a plastic symphony verging on abstraction.

After having worked and lived with Van Gogh in Provence, Gauguin was to flee to Paris which he left fairly soon to take refuge in Tahiti, the wonderful island in the South Seas. His was a voluntary exile, an attempt to run away from the false and easy symbols of civilization, a quest for a simpler way of life.

As he was convinced that art ran the serious risk of becoming a mere outward appearance and thus prejudice immediate expression, he dreamt of a kind of art that would ignore every possible school device. He was not the first painter to break with the old continent: Delacroix had gone to Algiers and, albeit in a remote way, the Impressionists had an admiration for the Japanese. From his first stay in Tahiti Gauguin

brought back a series of "wild and primitive" works, which was precisely what he wanted. The artist was enraptured by the classical beauty and the figures of the Tahitian women. In his pictures he accentuated their attitudes so as to gain a more striking expression. He went even further: in his desire to penetrate the very spirit of the natives he simplified the outlines of the forms and used wide strokes of almost violent colours.

In his painting *What ho, Are You Jealous?*, (1892, plate 34) or in *Annah the Javanese* (1893), he makes so bold as to use new daring tints and new colour schemes. Everything seems extremely instinctive but it is also conceived and constructed according to a simple but peremptory architecture. Moved by a religious feeling he expresses the beauty of the Polynesian race, a beauty that is as yet unspoilt. He bestows on his

34 – Paul Gauguin. *What ho, Are You Jealous?* – 1892. Pushkin Museum, Moscow.

35 – Paul Gauguin. *The Dream* – 1897. Courtauld Institute Galleries, London.

36 – Paul Gauguin. *And the Gold of Their Bodies* (detail) – 1901. Musée d'Orsay, Paris.

landscapes a sort of slightly barbaric sumptuousness where he alternates harmonies of blue, Veronese green and pure vermilion, which frame orange, or amber-coloured nudes with olive-green reflections. His nudes resemble some primitive idols solemnized by their very simplicity, wide-shouldered, narrow-hipped and big-footed feminine figures endowed with a supple and composed grace. We are very far from European aesthetics. In *Two Tahitian Women* (1899, plate 32), the faces are accurate, with wide close-set eyes, slightly flat noses and fleshy lips. This picture of the two young women offering flowers becomes that of a primeval vitality well capable of soothing the artist, whose mind was constantly tormented even during his stay in Tahiti.

A torment which increases in *The Dream* (1897, plate 35), where the joy of painting has given place to an alarming art, made of somewhat oppressive harmonies. His return to Paris is a definite disappointment and he goes back for good to the South Sea Islands. Now his art no longer needs to resort to expedients. He draws the sense of the sacred from the mythologies of the forces of nature: the moon, the earth and the great creator of every thing, God Taaroa.

The spontaneousness of his nudes brings to mind some existential questions which are enclosed in the choice of a long enigmatic title for one of his pictures: *Where Do We Come From? What Are We? Where Are We Going?*, painted in 1897 (plate 33). Gauguin's paintings insist with agonizing strength on the eternal question of the mysterious relationship between man and nature. It is then that his anxiety will turn into vertigo. Gauguin was to write about this masterpiece: "Everything has been painted at one go, without any preparation, on a sackcloth full of knots and rugosities. The aspect is dreadfully rough, like a damaged fresco."

The tones range from light blue to Veronese green and for the nudes he has chosen a quite bold orange hue. Gauguin's concept joins the great tradition of mural symbolism, the art of the Egyptian temples and romanesque churches. If one looks at the picture from right to left, or from the foreground to the background, it becomes clear that the theme is the growth of the human condition, in its unity and its precariousness, between birth, love and death, centered on the mystery of our origin. In the middle of the picture stands the statue of the idol, a representation of the primitive tradition of the still untouched nature which Gauguin perceives in those faraway islands.

In his last pictures, *And the Gold of Their Bodies* (1901, plate 36), or *The Offering* (1902), the reference to the Quattrocento painters is obvious. Gauguin succeeds in making his plastically painted bodies emerge from coloured surfaces of an almost acid suavity.

During the winter of 1888, while Seurat was rising to notice in Paris and Cézanne was painting in his isolation at Aix, Vincent van Gogh (1853-1890) settled in the south of France where he intended to inquire into the light and colour typical of that area. Born in Holland, he had previously been a lay preacher in England and Belgium. His brother Théo introduced him to the Impressionists and he decided to become a painter.

After he had settled in Arles, he disclosed his ideas, his expectations as well as a desperate solitude, in a series of passionnate letters to his brother. In the same year he was to be admitted into a mental hospital after a fit of madness. In his lucid intervals he went on painting with an immense and feverish tension. He died during the summer of 1890, therefore his painter's career lasted for some ten years. Nowadays his pictures are familiar to almost everybody and some of them have become really popular thanks to the innumerable reproductions. This is precisely what he had wanted: an art which would be devoid of any highbrow implications, *joyous and comforting*.

After having assimilated the lesson of the Impressionists, he

37 – Vincent van Gogh. *Small Plaster Bust* – 1886. Rijksmuseum Vincent van Gogh, Amsterdam.

edged away in order to create an agitated painting, where every single stroke breaks up a colour which, applied in thick coats, vehemently underlines his passion and emotion. Van Gogh's main concern has never been an accurate representation of his subject. Shapes and colours are the means through which he expresses what he feels about things and through which he communicates. Just like Cézanne he has decided to give up "the imitation of nature". He does not blend with nature, he forces it to blend, to yield to the shape of his thoughts and to submit to his distortions. In a way he carries on the pictorial tradition of Holland, his native country, when he draws near to Rembrandt and Hals who, just like him, had a sense of light and a great concern for reality. He admires Delacroix's way of expressing colours, and Millet's social message. He considers the function of colour in a new perspective. He will then talk about using red and green to express man's terrible passions and will assert in different ways his love for yellow, which he considers as the symbol of faith and love. Van Gogh is certainly not a painter of nudes. He only painted a few, but they all have an undeniable strength about them. The theme of *Affliction*, a lithography of 1882, was born from his admiration for Japanese painting. "I must manage to draw a figure in a few steady

strokes, like the Japanese whose extreme neatness I envy",
he wrote in a letter to his brother.

The woman, holding her face between her hands, hides it
away from the spectator. Her body, rendered by a steady
stroke, is painted in profile. The *Naked Woman, Lying* on a
bed (1887, plate 38), turns her back upon the spectator. For
this body Van Gogh used white tinted with carmine, vermilion and grey-yellow. One of the reasons for which Van Gogh
cannot devote himself to the study of nudes in a extensive
way is his precarious financial situation. As he writes to his
brother: "I did not have the money to pay my models, other-
wise I would have devoted myself completely to painting the
figure."

Two years before he died he was to write to his friend John
Russell, the painter: "The painter of the future will be a
colourist, the like of him has not yet been seen." And again:
"I would like to paint portraits which, in a century's time,
might look like apparitions to the people's eyes."

He contrasts cognitive research and total clacissism with his
ethical research. Thus, if Cézanne's painting is at the root of
Cubism, Van Gogh's is at the root of Expressionism.

All things considered nudes require a plastic realisation

38 – Vincent van Gogh. *Naked Woman, Lying* – 1887.
    Private collection.

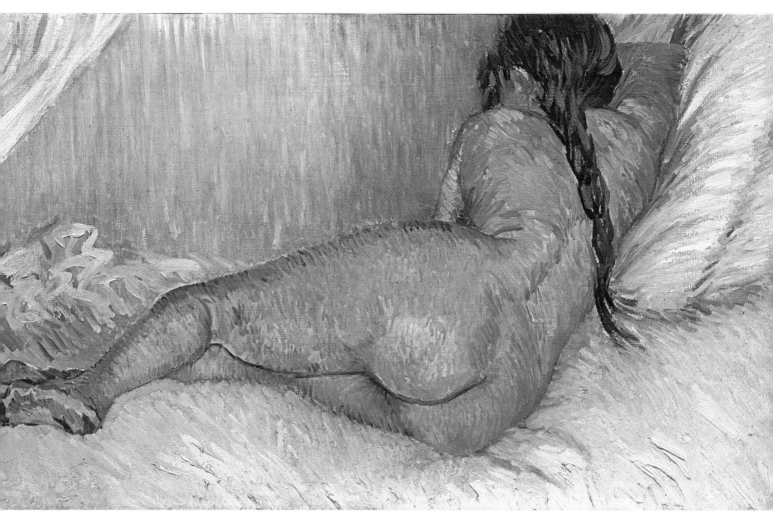

45

which, in a way, is contrary to the general rules of Impressionism. As a consequence Degas (1834-1917), although he remained apart and even separated from the so-called "Café Guerbois" School, offers an interesting case.

Of a classical mind – he always kept a copy of Poussin's *The Rape of the Sabine Women* in front of him – Degas was certainly not ignored at a time when Renoir, Pissarro and Sisley became famous. In his pictures the artist chooses to conceal his concern under composed subjects, apparently full of harmony. Throughout his whole life he was to remain isolated although – at the beginning – he had impetuously adhered to the innovations in painting.

At that time numerous Japanese prints were available in France where they had arrived thanks to the commercial relations that had been established with Japan. The first to collect them were the artists who gravitated round Manet. The Japanese masters delighted in representing the unusual aspects of the world which surrounded them. The novelty resided in the manner in which they represented the figures: in vista or on the edge of the print. Degas was most of all charmed and struck by this bold way of evading the fundamental rules of European painting. Why should a picture inevitably show an entire figure or a good part of it?

Thus, on the basis of that reasoning, he was to give a great importance to space and to the solid aspect of the bodies seen from unusual viewpoints.

Renoir had elected to depict the naked woman in a static attitude of repose. His models are practically always sitting or lying, with the exception of *The Large Bathers*.

For his part Degas interprets movement, he tries to fix poses and gestures and, to this end, he chooses the ballet.

Looking at them from above the stage he depicts the ballerinas while they are resting, at the end of the lesson, or during the performance.

The illusion which the ballet had created then gives way to creatures who no longer hide their tiredness. Degas strives to seize the principle of accurate movement, as if it were a snapshot, and reduce it to an artistic expression.

Right from the start, as in *Young Spartans Exercising* (1880), he tries to renovate a historical theme by introducing the aspects of the surrounding reality. Indeed he treats that classical theme with great realism, without idealizing the bodies which clearly represent those of his models.

In *Girls Combing Their Hair* (1875-76, plate 39), he lays the stress on the characters, particularly on the study of a figure seen from three different viewpoints. He voluntarily excludes

39 – Edgar Degas. *Girls Combing Their Hair* – 1875-76.
The Phillips Collection, Washington, D.C.

40 – Edgar Degas. *After the Bath* – 1885. Private collection.

41 – Edgar Degas. *Woman Combing Her Hair* – 1887-90. Musée d'Orsay, Paris.

the horizon by leaving it out of the frame, thus making the scene difficult to situate. The colours, whose excess of oil he has suppressed, become opaque and less suitable to blurred effects.

Degas associates the representation of the nude with the moments of privacy in a woman's life and captures her when, sure of being alone, she tidies herself. The woman has now forsaken all manner of affectation and he can "pinpoint" her while she is wiping her feet, washing with a sponge, laboriously combing her hair or wiping her body with natural gestures.

Such a conception of the nude, so distant from what a long tradition had established, could not but shock the public who, in 1886, had flocked up to see the Impressionists' last exhibition where Degas showed a series of pastels which he had indeed entitled *Women Bathing, Washing, Drying, Rubbing down, Combing Their Hair and Having it Combed*. He was accused of representing the feminine body in too crude a way. Degas's works reveal his passion for the study of the human body. In his pictures the human being acts or rests after an effort. Other artists before him had pursued the study of human anatomy: Michelangelo, so as better to depict a suffering and tormented human nature, and Raphael, whose wish was to create a world of harmony and beauty.

For Degas this study becomes the means of solving plastic problems, by representing reality. In his pastels, the diffuse light which filters through the curtains bathes everything. The armchair in which a woman is sitting becomes an effect of contrasts and tones; a towel, an iridescent group of colours, like the clouds at sunset.

In his last compositions Degas lets his true passion for colour

44 – Edgar Degas. *Woman Drying her Neck* – 1898. Musée du Louvre, Paris.

research take the best. He ventures extremely bold combinations: russets lightly touched with pink shades, variations in yellows, mauves and greens. He then applies his pastel which he fixes with hachured lines. When you look at them closely these pastels never result of one single colour: they are a set of lines and dots which give the surface an extraordinary vibration.

In his picture *Woman Drying her Neck* (1898, plate 44), the curves of the body are set off by an extremely different background. The arm, which seems to become knotted round the head, synthesizes the contour line in a modulated rhythm. In that composition the pastel variations attain an incomparable richness of colours.

The miracle of that art – the result of long studies and meditations – is the sensation of freshness and litheness it conveys, both typical of improvisation. His drawings are far from evoking the voluptuous tentations to which painters like Watteau, Géricault or Ingres had succumbed. His work requires meticulous preparations, a thorough study of the details and of the ensemble, a constant practice repeated a thousand times.

On the same canvas, on the same cartoon, the artist often uses different techniques: oil-painting, pastel, tempera. Degas associates all sorts of techniques with the powder of his pencils and he obtains new tonalities, of a classical purity. No one before him had ever dared to do that. As in a sequence of cinema frames, his pastels give life to a whole series of typically feminine attitudes, joyous and totally natural.

"It is no longer the flat smooth and always naked flesh of the goddesses..." writes Henri Hertz in his essay on Degas, "it is

45 – Henri de Toulouse-Lautrec. *Woman Pulling up Her Stocking.* Musée Henri de Toulouse-Lautrec, Albi.

47 – Henri de Toulouse-Lautrec. *Woman at her Toilette* – 1896. Musée d'Orsay, Paris.

the undressed, the real, the living flesh, a flesh that has been chilled by ablutions, whose cold granularity will soon smooth down." The figures of the *Luncheon on the Grass* or *Olympia* are posing. Degas disarticulates, breaks the continuous rhythm of the line, or prolongs it beyond the customary limits. Henri de Toulouse-Lautrec (1864-1901) is a disciple of Degas's. He too had learnt from the Japanese prints that the work could gain in persuasive force when relief and other

such details were boldly simplified. Lautrec's art has a tendency to capture, beyond the appearances, the true character of a maskless human being, a cruel exasperated character.
His pictorial methods are the result of direct experience. Unlike the Impressionists he does not strive to capture the changing effects of light; what he wants to do is to condense the expression in a few strokes by over-simplifying the sight. Crippled by a bone disease, Lautrec precociously revealed

48 – Henri de Toulouse-Lautrec. *Lechery* – 1896. Lithography.

his inclination for drawing. After watching a show at the Elysée-Montmartre, he tried to depict the global movement of the ballet. Then it was the turn of the Moulin Rouge whose director commissioned a new poster for his theatre. From 1894 on he devoted himself to painting the world of prostitution and especially that of the "maisons closes" (brothels). Lautrec liked the pale carnation of the young women who worked there, he was moved by their heavy bodies. For a certain period these women became his favourite models. He depicted them without any ambiguous feelings, any sensual evocation, he was merely interested in their existence and made no reference to their activity. He spent whole days in those places, watching, sketching, representing, without any dramatic or moral implications.

"A model is always frozen", he observed, "on the contrary they are alive." These young women are for him a source of

49 – Odilon Redon. *Cyclops* – 1895-1900. Rijksmuseum Kröller-Müller, Otterlo.

50 – Odilon Redon. *Woman and Centaur* – 1900-10. Private collection.

51 – Odilon Redon.
Pandora – 1910.
The
Metropolitan
Museum of Art,
Gift of
Alexander M.
Bing, New York.

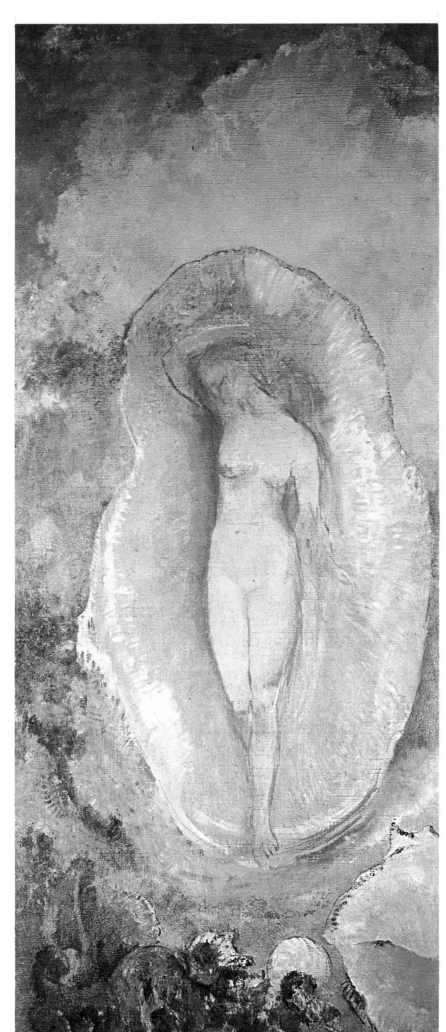

52 – Odilon Redon.
*The Birth of
Venus* – 1912.
Former collection
Stephen Higgons,
Paris.

true inspiration. They present a picture of free nakedness which he can fix in a plastic representation. The women he depicts in such surroundings go far beyond their condition, they assume a universal meaning.

The large-size picture *In the Salon, Rue des Moulins* (1894, plate 46) is a synthesis of numerous studies which Lautrec had made of this world. The picture represents the inmates of a brothel, whose indifferent bodies, sitting or slouching on a sofa are depicted in back view or in profile, while the fully dressed figure of the madam stands out from the uniformity of their group. These women do not offend or scandalize the eye. Who indeed could distinguish certain portraits of prostitutes from other portraits which Toulouse-Lautrec has left us? He is passionately fond of red-haired women with a white complexion. His favourite models are always remarkable for their fine heads of hair. This can also be seen in one of his last paintings *Woman at her Toilet* (1896, plate 47).

The numerous nude studies which he did in his studio date back to the same year. In those works the sumptuousness of the strokes compensates for the undeniable spareness of the drawing. The flesh takes on a red and green marble sheen. In Toulouse-Lautrec's eyes the figure was the most important element, and he maintained that the landscape was secondary. Toulouse-Lautrec has undoubtedly provided the themes which were later on to become characteristical of the XIXth century and his lesson has not been forgotten, especially by the Fauvists who were to paint with colour only.

Odilon Redon (1840-1916) discovered the nude when he was over sixty and was enthralled by it. Owing to the fact that he had matured slowly and rather late in his years, this painter belongs to the generation of the Impressionists. He started from the characteristical positions of late Romanticism which his introversion and dreamy temper encouraged, but later on his culture developed in a fantastic and visionary direction. He was not adverse to the study of nature, indeed he went much further, bringing his symbolical language to a very high degree of lyricism. He had spent his youth in Médoc, at Peyrelebade, where his father owned some land. There he felt free, in perfect communion with nature.

The academy lessons, which he attended in his twenties at the Atelier Gérôme of the Ecole des Beaux-Arts in Paris, brought him to realize that his way diverged from official culture. As a reaction he enthusiastically devoted himself to charcoal sketching, with extraordinary results. In 1878, his first trip to Holland revived his love for Rembrandt's painting. He met Corot, to whom – in a way – he owes a debt, and became enthusiastic for Delacroix, the freedom of his paintings, his way of using colours. Later on, in Paris, encouraged by Fantin-Latour and making use of his friendship with Armand Clavaud, a scientist and a highly educated man, Redon turned his charcoal drawings into etchings which were to become his main activity until 1890. He bestows the results of his cultural experience on these black and white creations: he

indulges in the wildest fantasy, freely drawing from the pictures and the symbols from different cultures and civilizations. He looked for life everywhere. Relentlessly, during the so-called "black" years, life would reveal itself to him in pictures that are often full of anguish or lost in insuperable gloom.

However, the "black" world disappeared when Redon found the peace of mind he had always yearned for, in the affections and the balance which often accompany mature age. It is a crucial step: Redon frees the world of his thoughts from the domination of anguish and transfers it to his pastels and oil-paintings. And he discovers colours. The mystery remains, the nightmare vanishes. In 1898, the picture of the *Cyclops* in the picture which bears the same name (plate 49), takes us back to the disturbing atmosphere of the black years. However, the figure of the naked woman lying among the flowers is a tangible sign of the transformation which has taken place.

Redon has just conquered light. And the flowers, those represented in this picture and those which are the protagonists of his paintings, confirm the deep suggestion and the evocation of the spirituality of nature.

"It is the joy of bright daylight contending with the sorrows of night and shadows, like the joy of a better feeling coming after anguish." This is what he writes in the years when the joyous deliverance he feels expresses itself in sudden chromatic ascents which create a rare brilliancy on his canvas.

The harmony of the body now appears to him as splendid and mysterious, like that of the world of nature. His picture *Eve* (plate 53) dates back to 1904: from the woman's bust, painted in warm golden tonalities, there emanates a delicate sensuality, in harmony with the spiritual atmosphere which seems vibrant with indistinct suggestions. *Pandora* (1910, plate 51), just as *The Birth of Venus* (1912, plate 52) also radiate a delicate and at once remote beauty.

If his nudes are immersed in a tangle of vegetation with which they seem to blend, it is due to the fact that Redon used to set them "in an Eden made for looks which are not ours but those of an imaginary world created by the artist, in which springs up and develops a beauty which could never be indecent ."

Redon's vision now acquires a typically Mediterranean stamp, a print whose lights and colours are unmistakably those of the South of France.

The refined elegance of the lines, the richness of the colour that is concentrated in iridescent sparks, are undoubtedly the pictorial equivalent of his intuition of the beauty and magic of the world, and also reflect the need he had to illuminate every physical image with a special light. Thus, until his death, in 1916, he will remain true to himself, and the vital harmony which pervades his very last compositions bears witness to the extraordinary journey made by the artist – of course – but above all by the man.

53 – Odilon Redon. *Eve* – 1904. Musée d'Orsay, Paris.

Editor in chief Anna Maria Mascheroni

Art director Ettore Maiotti

Layout Barbara Ravera

Text Gabriella Pavesi

Translation Pierre Remords

Production Art, Bologna

Photo credits Gruppo Editoriale Fabbri S.p.A., Milan

Copyright © 1991 by Gruppo Editoriale Fabbri S.p.A., Milan

Published by Park Lane
An Imprint of Grange Books Ltd
The Grange
Grange Yard
LONDON
SE1 3AG

ISBN 1-85627-229-X

This edition published 1993

Printed in Italy by Gruppo Editoriale Fabbri S.p.A., Milan